The Monster YOU Created:

Donald Trump

A Tale of Horror, Hate, and Trolls

From Hyde Park Publishing

Copyright Notice:

Table of Contents

Publisher's Note 5

Who should read this book.. 6

Introduction 7

The Mission: Crisis Negotiation Training 8

The Mission: Why It's Important 10
    The Lesson in the recent Brexit...11
    Clinton's Weaknesses...12
    What Wall Street Says...13

Interacting with the Real World..14

Trump VS Clinton 15
    The Woman Card 15
    Clinton vs Trump – Reality of the Female Vote 16
    Trump on Clinton and Guns and Violent Criminals...18

The Iran Deal 20
    Hundred Billion Dollar Giveaways 21
    What Do "We" Get From This Deal? 22

Trump vs Mexico 23
    Trump's Anti-Mexican Immigrant Rhetoric 25
    A Comparison Worth Reviewing...26
    Birthright Citizenship...28
    That Wall Mexico Won't Finance..29
    Trump Claims a Mexican Immigration Conspiracy...31

Trump #1 of All Time 33

Trump Vs Amazon.com...35
    Amazon and Tax Policy...35

Trump vs Facts 38
    Trump's Libyan Lie 39
    Trump's Black and White Lie 40
    Trump's Russian Affair 41
    Donald Trump, aka John Miller, aka John Barron..42
        A Joke Gone Awry...43
        A Double Persona – Who is John Barron? 44
    The Wrap-Up on Lies 45

Trump and Twitter 46
    Accidental Racism? Unlikely. 46
    Great Vox Article 47

Crazy Things Trump Believes 48

Global Threat #3...51

EIU Trump Threat Analysis 52

Trump and the mob 54

Trump's Campaign Filings 55

Trump Game 56

Trump Game Answers 57

Final Thoughts 58

Publisher's Note

We at Hyde Park Publishing know that spending your time reading about Donald Trump feels like a big waste. Heck, while researching this book and crafting the chapters, we wanted to throw our hands up in defeat and just quit.

But that is exactly why we persevered.

Donald Trump is a real world, actually running, top choice candidate for one of two major parties in the United States of America. All of those times you laughed at something he said, rolled your eyes in disbelief, and then changed the channel, you helped him get one step closer.

There are millions of Americans who are voting for Donald Trump. Some because they believe what he is saying, some because they think it's funny, and some because they don't care. All of those reasons are very dangerous.

He really does stand a chance at becoming President of the United States. The United States does stand a chance of electing him. And that is why we couldn't quit researching and drafting this book.

Regardless of your political affiliation, it's hard to imagine any sane, compassionate, and reasonable human being would agree with Trump's rhetoric and stump speeches. However, again, he garnered millions of votes during the Republican primary.

So we hope you read this book, collect the facts, and help in the battle to save our country from a seemingly crazed celebrity who has very little experience in the real world.

Thank you,
Hyde Park Publishing

Who should read this book

This book is not just for Liberals looking for self-assurance they are correctly viewing the political landscape in America. This book should be read by every registered voter in the United States of America. This book should be read by anyone who interacts with a registered voter in the United States of America. This book should be printed up and shared with random passersby on random streets in random towns in every state in the United States of America.

Why?

Because this book attempts to uncover a very clear thread in Trump's style – he has strained relationships with reality and truth. The text herein is meant to expose some of Trump's more enduring falsehoods, and present the only thing that can defeat him – facts.

Trump is very quick to jump on criticizers. He says they are nasty, mean, gross, disgusting, and many other words. His soft feelings are hurt any time someone has anything constructive to say, and this from the man who viciously attacks any and every person/group/association/etc. that he can target to get more free media time.

You should read this book, if for nothing more than to atone for the sin of allowing Trump to rise.

Yup. It's your fault. You allowed the Media to spoon-feed you the reality-TV crap Trump has been serving.

It's common for people to blame the Media for covering Trump and his antics – but they only cover him because you watched...religiously and loyally...like some brainwashed cultist. You worshiped at the altar of his particular brand of crazy. You are to blame for the billions (with a B) of dollars of free advertising and screen time that he has received.

Now it is your responsibility to marshal your facts, as well you can, and fight the good fight against the real life "He Who Should Not Be Named." The "Darkness from Manhattan."

Carry on soldiers! Fight with us to save our country against the bastions of misinformation, misogyny, and epic levels of racism. Take back our political system.

Introduction

Donald J. Trump, the self-purported, self-made billionaire.

Well, there isn't much to say about this newly minted political figure that he hasn't already said about himself.

From insinuating the size of his penis on a national debate stage, to mocking people with disabilities, Donald Trump has defied all reasonable expectations placed on someone running for President of the United States.

At every turn, Donald Trump has slipped free from every recrimination tossed his way, no matter how much it should stick. He defies the logic of politics, and he defies the laws of physics. And perhaps those very traits are what make him a seemingly untouchable force in American politics.

While Donald Trump lives in another dimension, closely connected but not entirely based in our own, he cannot be the next Leader of the Free World.

Yet, as proven by the June 2016 "Brexit" vote, when the wrong demographics are energized, their will can be forced on the vast majority of logical citizens. Donald Trump, whose core followers exhibit the same vein of concentrated fervor, is a real threat to the United States. His policies, beliefs, and selfish nature would do real and lasting damage.

The following pages are meant to help you, a hopefully sane human being, refute the talking points of those who have fallen under the Trump spell (or was it curse?).

This book is broken into sections like "Trump vs the Media" and "Trump vs Mexico." Each section contains information on the common themes, as repetitive as they are, found in Trump's public statements. Those themes are typically based on incorrect statistics, and are at times completely fabricated commentary.

By reading this book, you will gain a clearer understanding of what sort of political nightmare Trump is and would be to the United States, and hopefully you will be inspired to actively participate in the re-education of those Americans still tempted to vote for Donald J. Trump.

And you can always cite this book as a source if it helps (though most Trump supporters would unlikely treat this book as a primary source).

The Mission: Crisis Negotiation Training

Encountering a Trump supporter in the real world can be a shocking experience. While you know that these people exist, as millions of them have voted for Trump, you never quite believe in them until you are face-to-face (like zombies). These individuals cross the boundaries of all creeds, ethnic groups, and economic statuses. You must be ready at a moment's notice. Gird your loins (which, by happenstance, is a biblical phrase which means to prepare to do something difficult), and make a difference in the world!

The first chapter of the book is meant to help you negotiate the delicate task of interacting with a Trump supporter. Each additional chapter or section is focused on providing you the information necessary to arm yourself.

Follow these simple steps to ensure you, as successfully as possible, plant a seed of truth in the supporter's fallow field of Trumpian facts and figures.

The key component to this chapter, the *Behavioral Change Stairway Model,* is taken from manuals on crisis negotiation. This model was developed by the FBI. These techniques have been used in hostage and terrorist negotiations.

The *Behavioral Change Stairway Model* is laid out below:

The model is available for free to anyone who would like to study its inner workings.

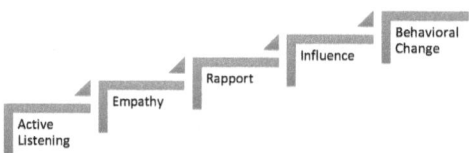

Not only can this model be used in terrorist and crisis negotiations, it is good at helping parties work through various disagreements and issues.

Advanced techniques to keep in mind include:

- Start by staying calm. Breathe with purpose.
- Fully understand their point of view. Use the "Five Whys" technique often used in business Six Sigma projects.
- Start by offering the truth as a question, meant for discussion and discovery, rather than a solid fact that must be accepted.
- Small wins grow over time.
- Manage the stress of the situation.
- If the outcome is less than you had hoped, learn from the experience and try again when the moment is right.
- Observe and control your own biases. One well-known Trump supporter is a Medical Doctor, after all.

The Mission: Why It's Important

He could win; no really, he could win.

That is what makes this book so disturbing. Trump, with all of his offending, bragging, and alienating, still has a chance of winning the general election and becoming the President of the United States.

Your help is needed in steering the Trump supporters, or near-supporters, in your life away from a decision that could lead to an utter collapse of reality; or at a minimum an economic, political, domestic, and international disaster. The morally elite in your life may also need a reality check. People who use phrases like: "I'll hold my nose when I vote"; "...the lesser of two evils"; or "Maybe America deserves Trump as President. That's the only way things will get better," are a real and present danger to the future of your country.

The United States, and even the world, cannot suffer a President Trump. The consequences would be long-lasting and devastating. This chapter will illustrate why counting Trump out is a bad idea.

Pundits and strategists, bloggers and media outlets have spent a lot of time printing and posting articles since the Brexit vote results came in. Those articles have primarily focused on how the Brexit has no direct parallel with the Presidential election in the United States. However, much of the messaging from the Pro-Brexit politicians and supporters in England echoes several common themes being used in the U.S. Presidential election.

In Trump's own words, he tied Brexit directly to the U.S. Presidential election:

> *"Come November, the American people will have the chance to re-declare their independence. Americans will have a chance to vote for trade, immigration and foreign policies that put our citizens first. They will have the chance to reject today's rule by the global elite, and to embrace real change that delivers a government of, by and for the people."*

British voters delivered a crushing rejection to the establishment. That is Trump's message.

The BBC published an article, prior to the Brexit vote, which listed 5 issues that are similarly at stake between the two topics; Brexit and the U.S. election.

- An angry electorate
- Globalization
- Immigration
- Lost Pride
- Populism

Sound familiar?

There is a growing sense of despondency and anger among citizens. A large percentage of voters agree with the sentiment that the economy is rigged in favor of the corporate elite and super-wealthy. These feelings have also been directed at minorities and religious groups. When you consider the issues of terrorism and police action, a polarizing effect has encumbered the United States. Important issues, like gun control and racial inequality in the legal system, are going no where in the political landscape – making no headway for remedy.

Mainstream Christian groups have related feelings of persecution due to, in part, the LGTB Rights movement (and the legalization of gay marriage). These sentiments, along with other hot button issues, have created a petri dish with just the right medium to foster growing angst.

A significant component of that anger, beyond domestic issues, includes the global economy. A major part of the Trump platform hinges on the mantra that Americans have lost millions of jobs, and trillions of dollars, due to bad trade deals. Deals that give other countries a better competitive advantage over the United States. American isn't winning, as Trump says, because it isn't self-focused any longer.

The issue of anti-globalization also embraces a glowing ember ready to ignite racial and national divides. Trump started his campaign with commentary on immigration. He has fostered and promoted the conversation that the United States are overrun with immigrants. He states that immigrants (mostly the illegal ones) who are coming across our borders (from the south or from overseas), are terrorists, rapists, and thieves.

So while it is convenient and easy to quickly dismiss the results of the Brexit vote as non-influential, that simply isn't the case. The components of the argument which motivated voters to ultimately agree with the Brexit are powerful, visceral, and dangerous.

As the BBC article said:

> "A victory for Brexit... by no means guarantees a Trump victory in the autumn. However, if the forces of disgruntlement, nationalism, populism and anti-globalisation are strong enough to force a radical move in the UK, they may be strong enough to force a radical election in America too.

Clinton's Weaknesses

While this book is not meant to enumerate Hillary Clinton's weaknesses as a candidate, it would be foolish to lose sight of her vulnerabilities. Clinton comes with a lifetime of public service. Part of that service is encumbered with rumors of scandals, back-room dealings, and a variety of personal attacks.

Her personal, professional, and political weaknesses are not small. When a Clinton falls down, they fall spectacularly; and on public display. Each time they get back up and soldier on, but the recovery takes a bit longer.

The Wall Street Journal published an article that showed Trump's path to a general election victory. The analysis was broken down into two paths:

The Florida Path and the Non-Florida Path

In short, Trump winning Florida (which has 29 electoral votes) would put him in good contention to snag enough electoral votes (supposing he won a few other key states). Without going into the electoral vote process (which would be a book on its own), a Florida win means Trump would have an easier path to victory. This is in addition to the states that he will win simply by being the Republican nominee.

Should Trump lose Florida, there is still a path for him to win. However, he would be pressed to pick up several more states, and that would prove more challenging.

Also, according to a Wall Street Journal / NBC News poll in May 2016, Trump led Clinton in the following areas:
- White voters (overall)
- White men with no college education
- White men with college education
- White women with no college education

The margin where Trump scored the biggest lead was with white men with no college education. Trump polled 48 points higher than Clinton with that demographic.

So while logic would lead a reasonable person to believe that Trump has no chance to win the election, the reality of the situation isn't so clear.

Some primary season math and key points to remember:

	Trump	Sanders	Clinton
Total Delegates	1,542	1,879	2,811
Popular Vote	13,300,472	12,029,699	15,805,136

- Sanders (who was purported to have fired up a political revolution) did not match Trump in the popular vote. Trump raked in well over 1 million more votes than Sanders.

- Trump had a "crowded field" to contend with, with tens of millions of votes going to other candidates like Rubio, Kasich, Cruz, and others.

Interacting with the Real World

Now that you have received some of the most advanced Crisis Negotiation training available (remember, it was developed by the FBI), and you understand that a Trump candidacy can still turn into a Trump Presidency, it's time to move into practical application.

The following sections are meant to provide you with facts, and some figures, that will help you navigate the hazy landscape and minefield you will encounter when speaking with a real-life Trump supporter.

As you read through these pages, and when you are called on to fight the plague of misinformation, just remember what these fine men and women said. Take comfort in knowing you are not the first to fight this battle.

> *"Nothing in all the world is more dangerous than sincere ignorance and conscientious stupidity."* - Martin Luther King, Jr.
>
> *"In politics stupidity is not a handicap."* - Napoleon Bonaparte
>
> *"Never attribute to malice that which is adequately explained by stupidity."*
> - Robert J. Hanlon
>
> *"It takes a great deal of bravery to stand up to our enemies, but just as much to stand up to our friends."* - J. K. Rowling
>
> *"Sometimes questions are more important than answers."* - Nancy Willard

Remember your training...

Trump VS Clinton

This first section is a quick look at how Trump prefers to take on his supposed opponent. While there is no way a published or printed resource like a book can stay up-to-date with the vagary of Trump's attacks against Clinton, this book is able to address a relatively recent (May 2016) attack chorus coming out of the Trump campaign.

The Woman Card

In early May of 2016, Trump continued his "woman card" attack on Hillary Clinton in an interview with CNN.

> *"She's playing the woman card, and if she didn't play the woman card, she would have no chance whatsoever of winning." Trump said.*

Trump continued by saying that Clinton's margins with women voters is not as strong as some believed. Some of his more unfounded comments included:

> *"Frankly, (Clinton) doesn't do very well with women."*

> *"I won with women by vast, vast majorities. I was way, way up with women far above anybody else in the exit polls..."*

In response, Clinton addressed Trump's comments with what became a popular sound bite. Clinton's reply also turned into a physical card that she markets as a "Women's Card" – which helped Clinton to raise more money.

As will easily become a trend later in this book, with closer inspection and scrutiny, one finds Trump's claims unfounded in reality. However, Trump is not without some merit with female voters. Trump won 57% of women voters in the New York primary, 55% of women voters in the Connecticut primary, and 54% of women voters in the Pennsylvania primary. Impressive, but the votes were in closed primaries, and the field of candidates for the Republican nomination had narrowed quite drastically.

RealClearPolitics.com published an article that outlined the gender-based results of seven well-known political polling groups from April 2016. Clinton beat out Trump in every poll, and by double digits in every poll save one.

Below is a chart of the polls and the lead Clinton had among female voters:

Poll	Clinton's Lead w/Female Voters
Investors.com	+15
RasmussenReports.com	+6
Suffolk.edu	+21
MediaRelations.gwu.edu	+19
NBCNews.com	+23
FoxNews.com	+22
CBSNews.com	+27

On average, Clinton trumped Trump by 19 points in each poll. Obviously this does not fit the Trump Campaign's narrative that Clinton does poorly with female voters.

Also, if past is precedent, Trump faces an uphill climb overall with female voters. In every election since 1992, female voters have cast the majority of their votes for the Democratic nominee.

Rutgers University's Center for the American Woman and Politics released a graph that showed female voters supported Democrats over Republicans by as much as 16 points (Clinton 1996) and as little as 3 points (Kerry 2004). While the Kerry lead with female voters is not as high as we see with President Clinton in the 90's, and Secretary Clinton in recent primaries and polling, it still stands that every election since 1992, the winner with female voters was still the Democratic candidate.

According to an April GWU/Battleground poll, Clinton scored a 51% favorable rating with female voters, while Trump scored only 26% favorable. Trump wins big with female voters, but only those who participated in his primary contests.

If Clinton holds the 19-point average polling lead over Trump with female voters, Clinton could receive the biggest voter margin among female voters since the time of her husband's presidency.

In addition to Clinton's polling lead with female voters, according to the Pew Research Center for U.S. Politics & Policy, 52% of all registered female voters are registered Democrats. Only 36% of registered female voters are registered Republicans. Even when Independent voters are factored in, female voters still lean heavily in the Democrat camp. And in a report from Rutgers

University's Center for the American Woman and Politics, the number of female voters has exceeded the number of male voters in every presidential election since 1964.

So to review:

- Clinton led in polls regarding female voter intention in the 2016 presidential election (by as much as 27 points in one poll).
- Female voters have voted for the Democratic candidate over the Republican candidate in every election since 1992.
- Clinton held a 51% favorability score with female voters, nearly 2 times as much as Trump's 26% favorability score with female voters in the same time period.
- Female voters overwhelming vote Democrat (52%) vs. Republican (36%).

Just because Trump has done well in his closed primaries does not mean he will perform better than Clinton in a general election.

Another favorite criticism of Clinton from the Trump Campaign includes a warning that Clinton wants to "abolish the Second Amendment," "take away all your guns," and "release all violent criminals from prison."

Clearly there is a difference between the conservative and liberal mindsets on the subject of gun control. As this book was being written, the Senate and House of Representatives Democrats were trying various tactics to get Republicans to take up gun control, in light of the Orlando mass shooting.

Mass killings, defined as the deaths of 4 or more people in a single incident involving a gun, have been on a steady rise in the United States in the past several years. The statistics, victims, and public opinion all seem to point to reasonable restrictions on guns (i.e. mental illness, suspected terrorists, etc.).

However, the topic remains a wedge issue out on the political stump.

Clinton's stance on guns is not to abolish the Second Amendment. She has supported a ban on assault rifles and other "military style" weapons. From Clinton's own website, she states:

> *"While gun ownership is part of the fabric of many law-abiding communities, too many families in America have suffered from gun violence. About 33,000 Americans are killed by guns each year."*

Clinton's website states she supports "sensible action" to address gun violence. The website lists comprehensive background checks, cracking down on illegal gun traffickers, holding dealers and manufacturers accountable when they endanger Americans, and keeping guns out of the hands of domestic abusers and stalkers.

To be more specific, Clinton calls for a strengthening of background checks and closing "loopholes" in those checks in the current system (i.e. the Charleston Loophole, television sales, internet sales, and gun show sales).

As for the Clinton will "release all violent criminals" component of this argument from Trump, the Clinton website addresses this topic as well. Clinton seeks to:

- "End the era of mass incarceration, reform mandatory minimum sentences, and end private prisons."

- "Encourage the use of smart strategies — like police body cameras — and end racial profiling to rebuild trust between law enforcement and communities."

- "Help formerly incarcerated individuals successfully re-enter society."

While Clinton does support a review of specific cases where someone is jailed unnecessarily, and she has supported some of President Obama's work in this vein, her main focus is on preventing these tragedies in the first place. Clinton's policies focus on ensuring the Justice system is improved, and that programs are in place to help reduce recidivism.

So to review:

- Around 33,000 people die of gun violence in the United States each year, and Clinton has called for gun control measures that are supported by a vast majority of Americans (including gun owners).
- Clinton has never called for the abolishment of the Second Amendment, or the ban of all gun ownership.
- There has not been a call or effort to take guns away from individuals, especially law-abiding individuals.
- Clinton has not indicated she would like to release all violent criminals from prison.

The Iran Deal

A frequent attack against President Obama from Trump focuses on the "Iran Deal." A culmination of negotiations with Iran to diplomatically reduce the country's attempts to gain a nuclear weapon.

For some context, the internet is full of videos where Republican leaders criticized the deal even before reading the text of the deal. And in March 2016, Trump continued his attack of the deal, while propagating misinformation.

Trump said, "...We give them $150 billion, we get nothing." In other comments he called the deal a disaster, and something that he would get rid of on day one. He also stated he would be able to negotiate a better deal for the United States.

However, the United States is not giving Iran $150 billion. Experts on foreign policy, including economic and political sanctioning of other countries, have disagreed with Trump's interpretation of the deal.

The first fact that requires clarity is where the $150 billion came from. The money was not paid from the US Treasury. Nor was it paid from the treasury of any other country. The money is Iran's money. As part of the crippling sanctions that have been applied to Iran in the past few years, the country saw much of its overseas money frozen. This is a common "first-step" in applying pressure against a sovereign nation with economic sanctions. When Russia was sanctioned for efforts in former territories, not only were large amounts of Russian assets frozen, but assets from key individuals in the Russian government also saw their overseas assets frozen.

It is also key to remember, in the case of Iran, most of the frozen assets do not belong directly to the government of Iran. A majority of the assets are from Iranian businesses. Some of those businesses may be controlled by the Iranian government (as is the case with the $2.3 billion owed to Iran from the oil and gas company Shell), but a good majority of the identified assets belong to commercial banks and other Iranian businesses.

A final consideration to keep in mind is that Iran will only have access to the assets identified as part of the nuclear agreement. Assets that are blocked due to terrorism or human rights violations are not subject to release under the brokered agreement. And some of the newly available assets will be given to creditors. A prime example of this is the $20 billion due to China from a deal made with Iran while Iran was under sanctions.

Economists estimate that Iran will receive approximately $60 billion. Other officials, like U.S. Treasury Secretary Jack Lew, have estimated the amount to be around $56 billion. Iranian officials have been quoted as estimating the number closer to $35 billion.

In each of those situations, the final tally is far off from the $150 billion payout that Trump infers the U.S. will be paying – perhaps by secured funds? Like a money order?

While the sticker shock value of a supposed $150 billion payout has everyday Americans alarmed, there are several benefits to the "Iran Nuclear Deal."

Iran is blocked from building a nuclear bomb

Trump's claim that there is no benefit to the deal, that it is a bad deal – a horrible deal – is political theater. The key benefit in the Iran Nuclear agreement is that the Iranian government will no longer push to develop a nuclear weapon. The deal also included provisions for oversight by non-Iranian watchdogs.

The U.S. brokered deal led to major restrictions and intrusive transparency into Iran's nuclear program.

In addition to the 'no bomb' provision, Iran has agreed to give up 14,000 centrifuges, used to enrich uranium. The country also agreed to hand over 97% of its stockpile of already enriched uranium, and slow production of plutonium. Iran will also dismantle its only plutonium reactor.

To ensure compliance to the terms of the deal, Iran also agreed to allow international inspectors to enter the country and implement monitoring programs for the Iranian nuclear program.

All of this was put in place and verified **prior** to lifting
sanctions and releasing any frozen assets.

So to review:
- Trump's statement about a $150 billion dollar give away to Iran is not true.
- The Iranian government will receive far less than the agreed to amount, due to the available assets, remaining sanctions for other serious concerns, and repayment of debt to other countries.
- The U.S. was able to broker a deal with many great provisions. And while you can debate if enough progress was made, the resounding opinion by diplomatic and nuclear experts is that Iran will not get to an armed state with nuclear weapons while the deal is in effect.

Trump vs Mexico

From his first speech as a Republican party candidate for President of the United States, to almost every interview he holds on national television, Trump usually has something to say about Mexico.

The comments range from attacking the Mexican government to attacking U.S. citizens who come from Mexican descent – and everything in between. The rhetoric has been impactful enough that the President of Mexico, Enrique Peña Niento has compared Trump's comments to those of Hitler and Mussolini.

Here is a list of statements or tweets from Trump about Mexicans or the Mexican government. This list is not exhaustive.

The Mexican Government:
- "They're [Mexico] sending people who have lots of problems, and they're bringing those problems with us [sic]. They're bringing drugs. They're bringing crime. They're rapists."

- "The Mexican government is much smarter, much sharper, and much more cunning. And they send the bad ones over because they don't want to pay for them. They don't want to take care of them."

In Response to questions asking for evidence that Mexicans are rapists:
- "Well, somebody's doing the raping...I mean somebody's doing it. Who's doing the raping? Who's doing the raping?"

Trump attacking Jeb Bush:
- Trump tweeted, and then deleted, this comment about Jeb Bush "#JebBush has to like the Mexican illegals because of his wife."

- Trump also said this about Jeb Bush for speaking Spanish at a campaign event "@JebBush So true. Jeb Bush is crazy, who cares that he speaks Mexican, this is America, English !!"

After being confronted about a situation where Trump supporters attacked a homeless man due to his Mexican heritage (The attackers broke the older man's nose, and they urinated on the man):

- "It would be a shame...I will say that people are following me are very passionate. They love this country and want this country to be great again. They are passionate."

Trump's Take on Crime Statistics:
- In yet another tweet, Trump said "Sadly, the overwhelming amount of violent crime in our major cities is committed by blacks and hispanics-a tough subject-must be discussed."

The Great Wall of Trump:
- "I will build a great wall – and nobody builds walls better than me, believe me – and I'll build them very inexpensively. I will build a great, great wall on our southern border, and I will make Mexico pay for that wall. Mark my words."

Trump has openly called for a rounding-up and deportation of all illegal immigrants and undocumented workers. The oft-cited figure when identifying how many people this will impact is 11.3 million people; 6 million of which are Mexican.

To put that into perspective, and this is not an attempt at comparing the plight of these two people (but it is an interesting comparison), the Nazi Holocaust resulted in the death of approximately 6 million Jews. And when non-Jew deaths are added in (e.g. Homosexuals, Political Dissenters, Ethnic Serbs, Slavs, Ethnic Poles, Romani People, Persons of Color, and more) the Nazi Regime killed approximately 11 million people.

While Trump is not advocating (at the time of publication of this book) for the death of 11 million illegal immigrants, it is interesting to note that the numbers fit so perfectly – Trump wants 11 million people moved out of a specific territory. That is how another leader began his rise to power – calling for the removal of specific minority groups and immigrants.

In *Mein Kampf,* Adolf Hitler declared that the German people needed "Lebensraum," or "Living Space." According to Nazi doctrine, displacement of a population (including killing members of that population), was a vital part of the plan to establishing Lebensraum.

The suggestion that Trump mirrors a Hitler rise to power is not something to easily dismiss. People often equate their rivals to Hitler, as Hitler is the most "evil" political figure that can be conjured to mind by the average American. However, with closer examination, it is eerie how closely Trump's own playbook mirrors that of Hitler's.

And for any readers wondering how any of this relates to Trump being anti-Mexican immigrant, the following are excerpts from Trump's "Core Principle 1" on his website compared against selections of Hitler's "25-Point Plan."

The Issue: Blame a specific group of immigrants for a nation's problem, and promise to eliminate that group of immigrants.

Hitler's Stance: In his 25-point plan, Hitler included the following:

- Point #4: Only a member of the race can be a citizen. A member of the race can only be one who is of German blood, without consideration of creed. Consequently, no Jew can be a member of the race.

- Point #7: We demand that the state be charged first with providing the opportunity for a livelihood and way of life for the citizens. If it is impossible to sustain the total population of the State, then the members of foreign nations (non-citizens) are to be expelled from the Reich.

- Point #8: Any further immigration of non-citizens is to be prevented. We demand that all non-Germans, who have immigrated to Germany since 2 August 1914, be forced immediately to leave the Reich.

Trump's Stance: In a variety of speeches (some referenced in earlier parts of this section), Trump has called on the mass deportation of Mexican immigrants ("illegals" as he calls them), and he has called for a ban on Muslims entering the nation. Trump has also called for varying degrees of lessening of other types immigration; even legal types of immigration. On Trump's website, he listed a significant tenant of his platform.

Core Principle 1 as: A nation without borders is not a nation.

Now, that tenant at face value does not seem too insidious. However, when reading further down the page where that vision is listed, there is an obvious tone of anti-immigration, with a surprising amount of focus on Mexican immigration.

Trump's site calls for:
- Triple the number of ICE officers.
- Enhanced penalties for Visa overstays.
- An end to birthright citizenship.
- A Federal requirement to hire American workers first before granting any visas.
- At the time of publication, his first point on immigration policy is to build a wall on the southern border of the United States. This is included with a call to have the Mexican government pay for the wall that his administration would build.
- Immigration moderation, which takes the form of a stay on "green cards" being given to immigrants until an employer has attempted to hire from American citizens first.

To review Trump's immigration policies, you can access the following website (active at time of publication): https://www.donaldjtrump.com/positions/immigration-reform

The Similarities:

Hitler	VS	Trump
Eliminate birthright citizenship. Only racial members can be citizens		Eliminate birthright citizenship. Does not define how citizens would be identified.
Citizens should be selected for employment opportunities. Policies to stem/curb immigration are suggested to enforce adherence.		Citizens should be selected for employment opportunities. Policies to stem/curb immigration are suggested to enforce adherence.
Future immigration is to be prevented.		Future immigration is to be "moderated" and taxed/fined.

So while Hitler went further and started to murder the immigrants and populations he did not want in his country, Trump has not fully expressed his plans for immigrants.

The comparison of Hitler vs. any other political figure is often used for shock factor. That is not the intent here. The intent is to show that there are substantive similarities in what Trump has called for, and what Hitler enacted. Hitler just took his policies to an abhorrent extreme, by killing the 11 million or so souls he did not want in his country.

One of Trump's older criticisms on immigration policy is the concept of Birthright Citizenship. Trump has stated that the United States is the "only ones" to have birthright citizenship. This point relates back to Trump's continued misinformation campaign regarding Mexico.

> Trump stated *"And by the way, Mexico and almost every other country anywhere in the world doesn't have that [birthright citizenship]. We're the only ones dumb enough, stupid enough to have it."*

Politifact.com researched the policies of other governments to find the true about birthright citizenship. Reporting in 2015, Politifact.com wrote that 33 nations have a birthright citizenship policy in one form or another. In addition to that fact, Mexico is one of those nations that offers birthright citizenship. This form of citizenship also exists in many other North and South American Countries. Birthright citizenship exists in Canada (which along with Mexico and the United States equates to a hefty majority of North America being covered with this policy – nearly an entire continent). Brazil, and nearly every country in Central and South America also operated with birthright citizenship policies and laws.

On his immigration policy website, Trump blithely mentions his famous wall. He writes:

> *"Mexico must pay for the wall and, until they do, the United States will, among other things: impound all remittance payments derived from illegal wages; increase fees on all temporary visas issued to Mexican CEOs and diplomats (and if necessary cancel them); increase fees on all border crossing cards – of which we issue about 1 million to Mexican nationals each year (a major source of visa overstays); increase fees on all NAFTA worker visas from Mexico (another major source of overstays); and increase fees at ports of entry to the United States from Mexico [Tariffs and foreign aid cuts are also options]. We will not be taken advantage of anymore."*

In his bid for the White House, Trump has consistently mentioned his desire to build this "Mexico-Funded" wall along the southern border of the United States. The belief is that a physical barrier would keep out any more illegal immigrants.

Now while this sounds like a reasonable and permanent solution, there are many factors that Trump doesn't address. There are more than 2,000 miles of United States-Mexico border. Trump addressed this in an interview with MSNBC in early 2016. He stated the wall will only be 1,000 miles long due to natural barriers. In that same interview, Trump said that the wall will cost $8 billion and will be 35-40 feet high.

The numbers appear to be easy, and most people who have built a fence in their back yard are likely willing to accept the wall as plausible. However, there are many factors that don't add up:

- There are land rights issues that would need to be dealt with. When building fencing along the border, complaints arose from private landowners regarding the intrusion onto private land. In addition, there is at least one Native American tribe that owns large areas of land that straddle the U.S.-Mexico border in Arizona.
- There are international boundary treaties that govern structures along the Rio Grande and Colorado rivers at the Mexican Border.
- Geographical impediments, like sand dunes and run-offs, would need to be overcome.
- There are over 50 species of wildlife that may be found along the U.S.-Mexico border in California and Arizona that are protected, endangered, threatened, or candidate species for protected status.

Yet the simplest fact is the cost. Trump has claimed he will only need $8 billion to build this wall of 1,000 miles. However, the United States built fencing between the years of 2006 and 2010. That fencing covered only 650 miles of the border, and nearly half of the fence was constructed out of blockade-like barriers that prohibit/limit vehicles from crossing the border but not pedestrians.

That fence, which does not fully stop illegal immigration, and covers only a fraction of the entire U.S.-Mexico border, cost the United States $7 billion to complete. That cost does not include maintenance and upkeep – which has been reportedly high due to people using wire cutters and other tools to cut holes in sections of the fencing.

Trump estimated his version of the wall would be built for $10 billion to $12 billion. This number is not feasible, just using what is known from building a fence along parts of that same section of the U.S.-Mexico border. And a key factor needs addressed; Trump wants a wall and not a fence. He has been clear that fencing does not work, and a wall is the only solution. This means the costs of building a wall versus installing a fence would be much higher.

Mexico Won't Pay

The cost and possible limitations aside, Trump's most popular sound bite regarding the wall is that he will make the Mexican government pay for the wall. However, current and former leaders of the Mexican government have been quite clear that Mexico will not pay for the wall.

- President Enrique Peña Nieto said in an interview that "there is no scenario" where Mexico will pay for the wall.
- Former President Vicente Fox responded to the same question, saying "I am not going to pay for that fucking wall."
- Mexican Presidential spokesperson Eduardo Sánchez stated that Trump's belief Mexico would pay for a wall "false." Sánchez also said of the concept, "It reflects an enormous ignorance for what Mexico represents, and also the irresponsibility of the candidate who's saying it."

In an ongoing escalation of rhetoric attacking U.S.-Mexico relations, Trump was asked for evidence of how the Mexican government is sending criminals across the border. Trump responded by saying,

> *"Our leaders are stupid, our politicians are stupid, and the Mexican government is much smarter, much sharper, much more cunning; and they send the bad ones over because they don't want to pay for them. They don't want to take care of them. Why should they, when the stupid leaders of the United States will do it for them? And that's what's happening, whether you like it or not."*

Trump also stated,

> *"The Mexican government forces many bad people into our country because they're smart. They're smarter than our leaders, and their negotiators are far better than what we have, to a degree that you wouldn't believe. They're forcing people into our country. ... And they are drug dealers and they are criminals of all kinds. We are taking Mexico's problems."*

There is no evidence to support this theory that the Mexican government is "dumping" its criminals across the U.S.-Mexico border.

Various fact-checker organizations have mentioned the example of Cuba, in 1980, sending undesirable citizens of Cuba to the U.S., including prisoners. However there is no evidence this has happened with Mexican immigration. In fact, Mexico to U.S. migration has dropped precipitously. Undocumented migration to the U.S. from Mexico dropped to a net zero in 2008, and has stayed at zero or below since.

The Video

Another small incident that points to a sense of fabricated controversy is the use of misleading imagery in a Trump TV ad.

In his first presidential campaign TV ad, Trump showed some misleading images of large groups of migrants at a border. In the ad, a voice says, "He'll stop illegal immigration by building a wall on our southern border that Mexico will pay for." The video shows large groups of people crossing a border, hastily and almost desperately fleeing.

But the footage, while it is insinuated as the U.S.-Mexican border, is actually of Morocco, Africa.

The footage is readily available on YouTube, and is from May, 2014. The official description of the video says it is from the Interior Ministry in Madrid. The footage shows an "onslaught of hundreds of migrants to the wall that separates the Spanish enclave of Melilla from Morocco." About 800 people were trying to cross the border.

Trump's campaign has since claimed that it used the footage on purpose, to illustrate a point. The full statement is shown below:

> *"The use of this footage was intentional and selected to demonstrate the severe impact of an open border and the very real threat Americans face if we do not immediately build a wall and stop illegal immigration. The biased mainstream media doesn't understand, but Americans who want to protect their jobs and families do."*

It is relevant to point out that the TV ad does not include reference to the source of the footage, a logo of the originating broadcaster, or even a time-stamp of when the video takes place.

Trump #1 of All Time

Whether it's comments about his intelligence, how much of a fortune he has amassed, or how great he has done making "deals" that help him "win," Trump's message is that he is on top of it all.

In an interview on CNN in 2015, Trump was bemoaning the Republican party leaders dismissing him as a serious candidate.

> "They like to say, well, we don't consider him a serious candidate. Why wouldn't I be? I went to the Wharton School of Finance; I was a great student."

> "I go out, I make a tremendous fortune. I write a book called The Art of the Deal, the number 1 selling business book of all time..."

Most of what Trump says is subjective; and due to that subjective nature, one can hand-wave the comments as truth with few provisos. However, when someone makes the claim that they wrote the number 1 selling business book of all time, it can be measured.

Trump did write a widely acclaimed and successful book. *The Art of the Deal*, published in 1987, was a sort of hybrid memoir/business insight book. The book offers readers a series of steps, 11 in total, for achieving business success.

The book spent more than 50 weeks on the *New York Times'* bestseller list, and sold widely.

Yet, while his book did achieve some notable success, it is hardly capable of claiming the title of number 1 selling business book of all time. That is where the data catches up with Trump's claim; and the data tells a very different story.

The clearest method of looking at a book's sales is to reference the Nielsen Bookscan data. Launched in 2001, the Nielsen Bookscan tracks the number of print copies sold of a book, regardless of edition, by major booksellers and outlets.

Since 2001, *The Art of the Deal* has sold around 177,000 copies in all editions (breakdown listed below). This is not unremarkable. Should the book you are reading now only sell a fraction of that number in its print edition, the publishers would be ecstatic. However, that number does not qualify Trump's claims.

Published	Binding type	Publisher	Sales since 2001
11/1/1987	Hardcover	Random House	17,000
1/1/1989	Mass market paperback	Random House	90,000
12/1/2004	Mass market paperback	Hachette Book Group	70,000

It is also important to settle on a definition of "business book," as the genre is pretty vague and encompassing of a wide array of subject matters. Business books include memoirs of famous or important business men, investment advice books, self-help books that focus on professional goals, the popular business fable (also called management fiction), and much more.

While Trump's book definitely fits into the realm of business book, to properly identify what fits in the genre will let one identify the true "number 1 bestselling business book of all time."

Below is a table of some very popular business books. Each of these easily fit into the genre, and each of these has sold more copies since 2001 than Trump's book. And when you compare these numbers to even the most liberal numbers associated with sales of *The Art of the Deal* from before 2001, Trump's book still fails to make the number 1 spot he claims.

Title	Published	Nielsen data (since 2001)
How to Win Friends & Influence People	1936	2.27 million
The 7 Habits of Highly Effective People	1989	2.18 million
Rich Dad Poor Dad	2000	6.99 million

Trump's book has done well since being published, but there are more than a few other business books that have sold even more copies, and are closer to claiming the number 1 bestselling business book of all time title.

Trump Vs Amazon.com

In mid-May 2016, Trump re-ignited an old assault on Jeff Bezos, founder and CEO of Amazon. The basis of the attack was Trump's outdated assumption that Amazon does not pay State taxes. Trump also claimed that Bezos purchased the Washington Post for lobbying power in Congress to protect an "Antitrust" that Trump alleges Bezos has in Amazon, and to continue paying no State taxes.

> *"Amazon is getting away with murder tax-wise. He's [Bezos] using The Washington Post for power so that the politicians in Washington don't tax Amazon like they should be taxed."*

> *"...he [Bezos] thinks I would go after him for antitrust because he's got a huge antitrust problem because he's controlling so much. Amazon is controlling so much ... and what they've done is he bought this paper for practically nothing, and he's using that as a tool for political power against me..."*

Amazon and Tax Policy

On the surface, Trump's claims against Amazon may seem realistic. American news outlets regularly run stories of CEOs and major corporations dodging tax liabilities through various loopholes in the tax code. This is a time honored tradition, one that even Trump has said he takes advantage of in his own taxes. Even Senator Bernie Sanders released tax returns during his campaign to run for President that showed the progressive, and self-described "Democratic Socialist," taking advantage of various tax deductions. This helped Senator Sanders bring his own tax burden below the national average for someone in his tax bracket.

The "everyone does it" mentality lends credibility to Trump's accusation. However, the attack is wrong. Not only does Amazon pay State taxes (where required), the company is lobbying in the other direction.

To start, Amazon did have an advantage for several years over the typical retail outlets. Physical retail locations, also called brick-and-mortar stores, have always been required to pay State sales taxes (where required by the State government). Online retailers like Amazon were able to bypass these taxes, as they were not physically located in the States.

State lawmakers saw this happening and began to change State law to include Amazon. Over 25 States, whose population covers nearly 80% of all American, require Amazon to enforce the collection and payment of sales taxes.

Due to this one-sided requirement, Amazon has actually begun lobbied to enforce the collection and payment of sales taxes for all online retailers. Amazon, as one of the largest fish in a very big pond, is forced to collect and pay sales taxes for the enforcing States, but many online retailers, and especially the Internet's version of "mom and pop" businesses, are not held to the same requirements.

In addition, Amazon paid over $270 million in income taxes in 2015. That equates to a much larger tax liability than is paid by other large U.S. companies (like GM which has had years where no income taxes were paid).

Trump's accusation of Bezos being politically motivated to buy the Washington Post is not fully developed. The challenge, and main inaccuracy, of Trump's assertion is that the U.S. Congress does not control the tax policy of individual states. Sales taxes are not collected at the Federal level. Sales taxes are only collected at the State level.

There are 50 States in the United States. A handful of those States do not collect sales tax of any kind. The States with no sales tax include: Delaware, Montana, Oregon, and New Hampshire. A fifth, Alaska, has no state-level sales tax but allows municipalities to impose retail-level taxes. That leaves 45 States with sales tax laws. As of publication, just over 25 States were requiring Amazon to enforce the collection and payment of sales tax. This means that Amazon is enforcing sales tax in over 55% of the States which require sales tax.

As mentioned earlier, Amazon's lobbying in this matter has been centered on fairly enforcing sales tax across the board for all online retailers.

While owning the Washington Post may give Bezos clout in the news that is reported by the paper, it is unlikely that the paper's supposed lobbying power of the U.S. Congress could prove powerful enough to lobby the members of 45 State legislatures on so specific an issue.

However, even though States set sales tax policies, there is some legal confusion over if the current tax code allows for taxation of online retailers. The U.S. Congress has seen legislation in the 2016 session that would specifically call out a State's right to collect sales taxes from the sales of online retailers.

Interestingly, the online auction site, eBay has fought this type of legislation. eBay is reported to have sent out tens of millions of emails asking for sellers to lobby their legislator to vote against the bill. Amazon, on the other hand, has supported unilateral legislation.

In 2013, Paul Misener, Amazon's VP of Global Public Policy, wrote to the Senate regarding the Marketplace Fairness Act. In his letter, Misener said "Amazon.com has long supported a simplified nationwide approach that is evenhandedly applied and applicable to all but the smallest volume sellers."

The bill currently being debated in the U.S. Congress exempts online retailers with less than $1,000,000.00 a year in sales from the provisions.

Below is an excerpt from NPR's Planet Money from 2013 under the Trade category; *"Why Amazon Supports an Online Sales-Tax Bill"* by Jacob Goldstein. The piece begins by explaining the responsibility of the buyer.

If you live in a State that charges sales tax **and** buy something from an online store that does not charge you sales tax, then you are required to calculate the taxes and add it to your annual State tax liability. The piece references reporting done that demonstrated very few buyers actually follow through with this requirement. Thus, most online shoppers have committed tax fraud without even understanding it had happened.

So why would Amazon support a sales tax measure? The article lists two reasons:

Reason #1
Collecting state and local sales tax all around the country would require a fair bit of effort on the part of online retailers, because sales tax rules vary from state to state. That's not a huge deal for a giant company like Amazon, but it would be more of a burden for smaller online retailers. From Amazon's point of view, that's a good thing — it makes life harder for Amazon's smaller competitors.

That's why big businesses, despite what they may say, often like regulations. They make life harder for small, would-be competitors. But in the case of Amazon, this argument is less compelling: Amazon spent years doing everything it could to avoid charging sales tax.

Reason #2
Under current law, Internet retailers have to charge sales tax in states where they have a significant physical presence — like, say, a big warehouse. For a long time, Amazon kept warehouses out of big states so it could avoid charging sales tax in those states.

Brick-and-mortar retailers didn't like this, and started lobbying state governments to push for Amazon to charge sales tax. So Amazon changed its strategy. The company agreed to start paying sales tax in more states — and it started building huge warehouses near major metropolitan areas in those states.

The warehouses meant the company had to start charging sales tax. But having warehouses closer to big cities also allowed Amazon to start offering same-day delivery to millions of customers.

As the FT reported last year, the brick-and-mortar stores got the level playing field they wanted for sales tax. But they also got a new level of competition from Amazon. If the company can make cheap, same-day delivery work, it will eliminate one of the last advantages of physical stores.

Trump vs Facts

This section could grow into an entire book. There is no shortage of material where Trump says something is true, and said something is not true. Many political candidates have misspoken, poorly relayed a statement, or said something that wasn't true. However, when confronted with fact-checkers and the truth, those candidates will apologize, restate what they meant, and move on. Trump does not restate, apologize, or move on. He will double down on the untrue statement, and seek to employ ad-hominem attacks to prove his point ("Little Marco," "Lyin' Ted," and so on...).

The following sections are some of Trump's more obvious lies. These are untruths that are easy to disprove. No complex analysis or massaging of statistics.

At the 2016 Republican Primary debate in Houston, Texas, Senator Ted Cruz tried a new line of attack by saying Trump was in favor of "Libya."

Libya, or rather the removal of the dictator Muammar Gaddafi from power in Libya, was an anti-Obama/Clinton talking point used by many Republicans in the 2015/2016 campaign cycle. Due to unforeseen consequences in the region, many Republicans equate the problems with the regime change in Libya (among other factors).

Trump's reply to Cruz's attack was pretty clear:

> *"He [Cruz] said I was in favor in Libya. I never discussed that subject. I was in favor of Libya? We would be so much better off if Gaddafi would be in charge right now."*

However, Trump had spoken at length about his views of Libya; and even more specifically, Gaadafi. In a 2011 video released by Trump from his office at Trump Tower (since deleted, but now resurfaced on Buzzfeed.com), he said:

> *"I can't believe what our country is doing. Gaddafi in Libya is killing thousands of people, nobody knows how bad it is, and we're sitting around we have soldiers all have the Middle East, and we're not bringing them in to stop this horrible carnage and that's what it is: It's a carnage."*

> *"Now we should go in, we should stop this guy, which would be very easy and very quick."*

> *"We should do on a humanitarian basis, immediately go into Libya, knock this guy out very quickly, very surgically, very effectively, and save the lives."*

This "misinformation" does include some mention of statistics; and of course those statistics are inaccurate. However, the real issue at hand is the fabrication of a reporting agency to lend credibility to the lie.

On Twitter, Trump posted an infographic that included some crime statistics. One of the statistics that gained a lot of attention was the assertion that 81% of white murder victims are kill by black people. The tweet also included a statistic alleging that 97% of all black murder victims are killed by black people.

Obviously these statistics aren't correct. Well over 80% of white people are killed by other white people. These are easily checked statistics – using sources like the FBI crime data reports. However, the real lie didn't come from statistics that could be distilled down to tell any story the teller wants proven.

The real lie was the alleged source of the statistics. Trump's infographic attributed its statistics to the "Crime Statistics Bureau of San Francisco."

No such organization exists.

Trump has claimed to know Russian President Vladimir Putin "very well."

> *"I got to know him very well because we were both on 60 Minutes, we were stable-mates and we did very well that night."*

In a Republican Presidential primary debate attempted to suggest that he and the Russian President are friendly. His basis for this assertion comes from an episode of 60 Minutes where both Trump and Putin appeared as guests on the same episode of the show.

The problem with this assertion is that Putin was interviewed for the show in Moscow. Trump's interview was recorded in his office in New York.

Both interviews were pre-taped, as 60 Minutes is not a live broadcast.

Trump may have met Putin at some other point, or during some other event, but Trump did not meet Putin because they both showed up to be interviewed on the same episode of one show.

However, as an aside, it does say something about the subtlety of the 60 Minutes producers to put these two men on the same episode of the highly regarded interview news program.

Donald Trump, aka John Miller, aka John Barron

In the 1980s and 1990s, Trump was going through public relationship troubles. Various women were in and out of his life. As such, Trump was in and out of various media outlets. Allegedly during this time, Trump frequently spoke with various reporters while pretending to be someone else. Even before the time of the "Great Tradition of Internet Trolling and Catfishing," Trump used such tactics. And while the concept of pretending to be someone else to get good press about oneself may seem like an insignificant faux pas, there is a deeper concern. Trump not only called media outlets and pretended to be someone else, but he admitted it and apologized. Yet now, decades later, he is refusing to admit up to the con.

In a world of self-promotion and Kardashians, it is not an unjust assumption to believe celebrity-hungry people like Trump use unconventional tactics to drum up public press and excitement. With a 24-hour news cycle, and an ever increasing demand for fresh scandal and content, many celebrities have hit the "big time" with little more than self-promotion and well-timed media hype. Trump has many failings as a potential presidential candidate, but he understands branding and monetizing one's assets.

In the early 90s, not long after his book "The Art of the Deal" was released, Trump was experiencing some buzz. In phone calls with media outlets, like People Magazine, Trump pretended to be someone other than himself. Using the names John Miller and John Barron (and this is where it gets confusing), Trump stated he was Mr. Trump's "PR guy" and spokesperson.

The Washington Post gained access to a recorded phone conversation, where a voice that many say is Trump is giving some very "Trump-like" responses to an interviewer's questions. The full transcript, and audio recording, is available online.

When Trump was asked about the newly-resurfaced recoding, he told NBC that it was not him and he had no idea what they were talking about.

> "It was not me on the phone. I don't know anything about it. You're telling me about it for the first time."

However, Trump did know about the incident. People Magazine printed a piece in 1991 that included an apology from Trump for the whole "John Miller" incident – as it was all a big joke.

A Joke Gone Awry

While 2016-Trump denies he was the voice in the recording, or that he went by other names when speaking with the press, 1991-Trump admitted to the deception.

Below is are a few short excerpts from the 1991 People Magazine article written by Sue Carswell. The full article can be found in the People Magazine archives on People.com:

> ...Just two weeks ago, though, Ms. Maples was not even taking The Donald's calls. Not after a PEOPLE reporter played her a tape on June 26 of a man saying that he was a Trump publicist named John Miller.
>
> A shocked, devastated Marla identified the voice as that of Trump himself. He announced, among other things, that he'd traded in his Georgia peach for an Italian model (Carla Bruni).
>
> "When I heard his voice on that tape saying those things, I said, 'Whoa! Uh-uh. No more,' " says Marla. "If he could say all that stuff and act like it's cool to have this playboy image, then oh my gosh, all I could say was, 'Baby, you're on your own.' "
>
> Meanwhile a penitent DonJuan-ald had come to the opposite conclusion. The John Miller fiasco he called a joke gone awry.
>
> "What I did became a good time at Marla's expense, and I'm very sorry," says the newly humbled tycoon.

Even with the public apology, and no resulting lawsuit at that time from Trump on mis-reporting by People Magazine, Trump continues to deny the incident (at time of publication).

In addition to the admission in the People Magazine article, Trump has provided testimony in a lawsuit that he has used a fictitious name in business dealings.

In the now remembered Undocumented Migrant Polish Workers employment lawsuit against Trump and his business for the Trump Tower project, Trump was asked if he had ever used the name John Barron.

Trump's reply, "I believe on occasion I used that name."

There is a long history of Trump using the name John Barron in personal and business dealings. It was reported (and mentioned in the 2015 Trump Biography "Never Enough: Donald Trump and the Pursuit of Excellence" by Michael D'Antonio) that Trump may have picked up this trick from his own father, Fred Trump, who sometimes used the name Mr. Green.

So who is John Barron?

According to various sources, John Barron (sometimes spelled Baron) has been reported as a Vice-President of Trump Organization, Trump Spokesman, Trump Executive, and Trump Representative. The earliest known article featuring this alternate identify of Trump's was in 1980 on the front-page of the New York Times. The name was spelled Baron in this article, and the piece directly covers Trump and his decision to destroy sculptures on a Fifth Avenue landmark building he demolished as part of the Trump Tower project.

John Barron appeared in New York magazine, The Washington Post, The New York Times, and other publications.

Trump has had an enduring fascination with the name. He has used "the Baron" as a codename for himself. He directed the writer of a TV series he commissioned about a New York real estate mogul to name the main character Barron. And most recently, he named his youngest son Barron.

Trump's tenuous relationship with true statistics and facts has proved non-problematic for him as a Presidential candidate. Contrary to most people's expectations, the more reporters and fact-checkers try to bring Trump down because of his lies, the more popular he seems to become. Each week brings more tales of fantastical statements made by Trump and his campaign surrogates.

And as Doyle McManus said in an LA Times Op-Ed about Trump's ability to lie and get away with those lies:

This campaign will be a test of Trump's own advice from his 1987 bestseller — and it really was a bestseller, no lie — "The Art of the Deal":

"You can't con people, at least not for long. You can create excitement, you can do wonderful promotion and get all kinds of press, and you can throw in a little hyperbole. But if you don't deliver the goods, people will eventually catch on."

It is just in America's best interest to figure out he can't deliver the goods, before he is elected into the most powerful office in the World.

Trump and Twitter

There is no doubt that Twitter has become a mainstream-campaign-message-delivery machine. Trump has used Twitter as his own personal platform, gaining an estimated $2 billion (with a B) of free media coverage – much of which comes from the mainstream media's fevered attention to Trump's Twitter feed.

Several media outlets and news organizations have begun to take a deeper look into Trump's Twitter feed, and the results are not surprising.

Accidental Racism? Unlikely.

In early July 2016, Trump posted an anti-Clinton infographic that offended a great many people.

While the immediate backlash against Trump posting a Star of David graphic on a pile of money can be attributed to "political correctness" or "unnecessary sensitivity" (which can be debated), the source of the image is far from politically correct.

Trump has a history of retweeting images, infographics, and tweets from organizations and individuals with incredibly racist or immoral leanings. The Hillary-Star-of-David-On-Piles-of-Money tweet is no exception.

This tweet originated not from Trump, but from another Twitter account ran by a self-described "comedian" who will offend you if "you are Liberal, Politically Correct, Feminist, Democrat." This Twitter account has created many racists and demeaning memes, including one where pictures of Clinton's face are placed in the shape of a swastika.

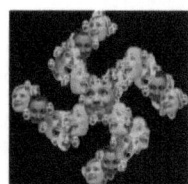

In one of the most thorough reviews of Trump's Twitter feed, Vox.com writer Zachary Crockett analyzed 2,500 tweets over a 7.5-month period. He filtered out retweets, quotes of other people, and links to other content. Crockett focused solely on tweets from/by Trump.

Crockett found several interesting points, and the article sports more than one high-quality infographics to help parse and explain the data. Among his observations, Crockett pointed out that Trump tends to be very negative on Twitter. While no one outside of the most severely devoted sycophant is truly surprised by this, the hard data is interesting.

According to Crockett's analysis, Trump is negative in 45% of his tweets. The newly minted politician is only positive in 28% of his tweets.

In addition to being negative in a majority of his tweets, Trump tends to use exclamation points quite liberally. Crockett reports that over 76% of Trump's tweets contain at least one exclamation point.

One more thing that Crockett reported, is that Trump spends more time on Twitter tweeting about the media than he does about important policy issues. Trump has 3.5 times more tweets about the media than he does about policy issues.

Media-related Tweet Mentions	Policy-related Tweet Mentions
• News: 139	• Immigration: 33
• Interview: 100	• Economy/Jobs: 29
• Ratings: 44	• Health care: 4

Crockett's analysis goes into more depth regarding additional findings, and is worth reading.

But beyond the Vox.com article, just a quick look at Trump's Twitter feed can prove just what sort of candidate he is for America.

Donald J. Trump ⊙
@realDonaldTrump

"@mplefty67: If Hillary Clinton can't satisfy her husband what makes her think she can satisfy America?" @realDonaldTrump #2016president"

4/16/15, 5:22 PM

Crazy Things Trump Believes

If you (or the party you are trying to help come to the light of reality) are not yet convinced, the following is a list of things Trump purports to believe.

All of these things can be found on his Twitter feed, in various interviews with media outlets, or in his own public addresses.

- Trump has stated multiple times that he, and hundreds of people who have contacted him personally to agree with his claim, that he saw thousands of Arab-Americans celebrating on September 11th, 2001. His accusation is that these people were celebrating that two planes flew into the Twin Towers, and the celebration was a public demonstration. There are no media reports, or recordings of media at the time, to support this claim.

- Muslim Mosques should be tracked and placed under surveillance by law enforcement officials. He also stated that all Muslims should be tracked via a government database, but has sense backed off some of those comments. Trump has stated that the Muslim community knows what is going on, and they should be watched.

- The United States should not only use waterboarding as part of interrogation, but more aggressive techniques should also be employed. His logic was that since the enemy uses beheadings, the United States should increase the intensity of its own practices.

  Specific quotes from Trump on torture/waterboarding include:

  "Torture works, ok folks?"
  and
  "I would bring back waterboarding and I'd bring back a hell of a lot worse than waterboarding."

- Trump has stated that "true" unemployment statistics put the rate well over 40%. That is a 30+ point increase over reported numbers.

- Climate change is a hoax, invented by the Chinese.

- Japan and South Korea should get their own nuclear arsenal.

- Doctors should be punished for administering abortions, and women who have abortions should also be punished.

- "ISIS is making a tremendous amount of money because of the oil that they took away, they have some in Syria, they have some in Iraq, I would bomb the sh-- out of them."

"I would just bomb those suckers, and that's right, I'd blow up the pipes, I'd blow up the refineries, I'd blow up every single inch, there would be nothing left."

- He's sexist:
  - About Carly Fiorina

    "Look at that face! Would anyone vote for that? Can you imagine that, the face of our next president? I mean, she's a woman...but really, folks, come on. Are we serious?"

  - About Megyn Kelly

    "She gets out and she starts asking me all sorts of ridiculous questions. You could see there was blood coming out of her eyes, blood coming out of her wherever. In my opinion, she was off base."

  - About Hillary Clinton

    "If Hillary Clinton can't satisfy her husband what makes her think she can satisfy America?"

  - "Heidi Klum. Sadly, she's no longer a 10."

  - "It must be a pretty picture. You dropping to your knees." Trump to Brande Roderick.

  - "[Ivanka] does have a very nice figure. I've said if Ivanka weren't my daughter, perhaps I'd be dating her."

  - "The Face of a Dog!" Trump regarding New York Times reporting Gail Collins.

  - "You're disgusting, you're disgusting!" Trump to a lawyer when she requested a break to go pump breast milk.

  - "I bet you make a great wife." Trump to a contestant on The Apprentice in 2005.

  - "All of the women on The Apprentice flirted with me – consciously or unconsciously. That's to be expected."

  - "You know, it doesn't really matter what [they] write as long as you've got a young and beautiful piece of ass."

- o "A person who is very flat chested is very hard to be a 10."

- o "I like kids. I mean, I won't do anything to take care of them. I'll supply funds, and she'll take care of the kids."

- "He's not a war hero." Trump on Senator John McCain.

  At an Iowa campaign event, Trump said McCain was only a war hero "...because he was captured. I [Trump] like people who weren't captured."

- Trump suggested doing away with the Geneva Conventions.

  "The problem is we have the Geneva Conventions, all sorts of rules and regulations, so the soldiers are afraid to fight."

- Trump believes he is the best person to advise him on foreign policy, saying: "I have a good brain."

- "The LGBT community, the gay community, the lesbian community — they are so much in favor of what I've been saying over the last three or four days. Ask the gays what they think and what they do, in, not only Saudi Arabia, but many of these countries, and then you tell me — who's your friend, Donald Trump or Hillary Clinton?"

- Trump on Ted Cruz's father, and how Cruz's father was likely involved with Lee Harvey Oswald.

  "His father was with Lee Harvey Oswald prior to Oswald's being – you know, shot. I mean, the whole thing is ridiculous. What is this, right prior to his being shot, and nobody even brings it up. They don't even talk about that. That was reported, and nobody talks about it."

- "It is better to live one day as a lion than 100 years as a sheep." A tweet from Trump quoting fascist Italian dictator Benito Mussolini.

- "We won with poorly educated. I love the poorly educated."

- "I could stand in the middle of Fifth Avenue and shoot somebody, and I wouldn't lose any voters, okay? It's, like, incredible."

- "The other thing with the terrorists is you have to take out their families, when you get these terrorists, you have to take out their families. They care about their lives, don't kid yourself. When they say they don't care about their lives, you have to take out their families."

Global Threat #3

A well-regarded organization which provides forecasting and advisory services for government officials has recently named Trump a Global Economic Risk.

Created in 1946, The Economist Group has worked with businesses, financial firms, and governments to provide information and forecasting of how the world is changing and how that change impacts various economies. A key component to The Economist Group is the EIU, or Economist Intelligence Unit. This group provides country and industry risk analysis. The research of the EIU works to provide insight into a global economy, with a network of highly specialized country-specific resources.

The EIU first named Trump to its Global Risk forecast in March 2016. At the time Trump was not high up on the list, as the assumed likelihood of Trump becoming President of the United States was very low.

However, now that Trump is the Republican Party Nominee, he stands a greater chance to achieve the Presidency.

The EIU has named Trump a greater threat to the global economy than China prompting a clash of arms in the South China Sea due to Chinese expansionism, the United Kingdom voting to leave the European Union (which happened), and the rising threat of Jihadi terrorism.

In fact, Trump winning the U.S. Presidential Election was listed as the 3rd greatest threat to the global economy.

The ranking of Global Threats has been listed below (as of 6/15/2016):

1. China experiences a hard landing
2. Currency volatility and persistent commodity prices weakness culminates in an emerging markets corpo
3. Donald Trump wins the US presidential election
4. Beset by external and internal pressures, the EU begins to fracture
5. "Grexit" is followed by a euro zone break-up
6. The rising threat of jihadi terrorism destabilizes the global economy
7. Global growth surges in 2017 as emerging markets rally
8. The UK votes to leak the EU
9. Chinese expansionism prompts a clash of arms in the South China Sea
10. A collapse in investment in the oil sector prompts a future oil price shock

The EIU released a statement for each of the 10 greatest global economic threats. The statements each include an analysis as to why the threat was assessed at its specific level.

The EIU listed "Donald Trump wins the US presidential election" as a High Probability, High Impact; Risk intensity 16.

The analysis pulled out several key themes from Trump's policies as problematic for the global economy.

- Trump's hostility to free trade
- Labeling China as a "currency manipulator"
- Middle East policies that would be a potent recruitment tool for jihadi groups
- Indifference to nuclear proliferation in Asia

While the analysis is a concise and well-written portrayal of what many experts are saying about a Trump presidency, the EIU's conclusion was easily the most poetic part of the entire publication:

> *"Although we do not expect Mr. Trump to defeat his most likely Democratic contender, Hillary Clinton, there are risks to this forecast, especially in the event of a terrorist attack on US soil or a sudden economic downturn. It is worth noting that the innate hostility within the Republican hierarchy towards Mr. Trump, combined with the inevitable virulent Democratic opposition, will see many of his more radical policies blocked in Congress - albeit such internal bickering will also undermine the coherence of domestic and foreign policymaking."*

Excerpts of the EIU Global Threat analysis of a Trump presidency are listed below:

- "The chances of Donald Trump, a businessman and political novice, winning the US presidential election has increased of late, after he was endorsed by the Republican establishment as the party's official presidential nominee..."

- "Although we still do not expect Mr. Trump to defeat Mrs. Clinton, there are risks to this forecast, especially given the terrorist attack in Florida in June."

- "Thus far Mr. Trump has given very few details of his policies - and these tend to be prone to constant revision - but a few themes have become apparent."

- "...he has been exceptionally hostile towards free trade"

- "...advocating the killing of families of terrorists and launching a land incursion into Syria to wipe out IS (and acquire its oil)."

- "...his hostile attitude to free trade, and alienation of Mexico and China in particular, could escalate rapidly into a trade war - and at the least scupper the Trans-Pacific Partnership between the US and 11 other American and Asian states..."

- "...would weaken efforts to contain Russia's expansionist tendencies."

- "...indifference towards nuclear proliferation in Asia raises the prospect of a nuclear arms race in the world's most heavily populated continent."

Trump and the mob

"There have been multiple media reports about Donald's business dealings with the mob, with the mafia. Maybe his taxes show those business dealings are a lot more extensive than has been reported."

Senator Ted Cruz (R-TX)

Quite a bit of research has been done in determining the extent of Trump's mob connections. There are several news reports and even an unauthorized biography of Trump's ongoing relations with Mafia-connected business and individuals. It is a well-known and accepted fact that construction and commercial developers in a 1980s New York City came with a certain amount of interaction with reported mob families. And while Trump was never charged with any illegal activity, there has been a steady stream of "Trump and Mob" links crop up over the past few decades. Trump's alleged and actual business interactions with mob-related characters are widely documented.

- Trump Plaza

  Trump awarded a $7.8 million subcontract to S&A Concrete. The company, at the time, was partially owned by Anthony "Fat Tony" Salerno. Salerno was the alleged boss of the Genovese crime family.

  In 1986 indictment charges against Salerno, Trump Plaza was specifically mentioned.

- Atlantic City Dealings

  In 1981, Trump leased a portion of land for a Trump casino from a company two mafia-connected men controlled.

  Trump eventually bought the property for the casino from a well-connected Mafioso, for $1.1 million in 1982. The amount of the deal was reported at twice the market value of the property. The property had been purchased in 1977 for $195,000.

  According to reports at the time, the Trump Plaza and Casino were built by two Mafia-owned construction companies.

To ensure a careful tenor is struck when writing about a lawsuit-happy man's connections to organized crime families, it is important to include a note that clearly states Trump has never been indicted or formally charged for his connections and associations (alleged or otherwise) with said organized crime families.

Trump has been subject to research, legal investigation and questioning, and inquiry from agents in private, public, and law enforcement organizations.

Trump's Campaign Filings

June 2016 was not a strong month for the Trump campaign. The organization filed Trump's May FEC spending report, and the numbers raised more than a few eyebrows.

Trump's May FEC spending report filing seemed to heavily favor Trump's own companies and organizations; companies and organizations which accepted large payments from the Trump campaign.

Trump's campaign paid the following amounts during the month of May, 2016 (and only May 2016 – these amounts do not include earlier months):

- $26,000 to Trump National Doral golf course
- $11,000 to Trump Hotel Chicago
- $99,000 to Trump Plaza
- $5k to Trump Soho
- $5k to his son's Trump Winery company
- $29,715.42 to Trump International Golf Club
- $423,000 for Trump's vacation home/golf course in Florida
- $520,000 to Trump Tower.
- $125,080.31 to Trump Restaurant
- and a whopping $4.6 million for use of the private jet he already owns

That adds up to nearly $6 million spent by the Trump Presidential Campaign solely at Trump-owned locations, and solely in the month of May.

Trump Game

In an attempt to bring levity and entertaining methods of educating any unknowing masses the readers may know, Hyde Park Publishing presents our very own "Trump Game!"

The rules are simple, read one of the statements from below out loud. Then have the other participant(s) guess who the quote is commonly attributed to, Adolf Hitler or Donald Trump.

Hilarity will then ensue (and hopefully some introspection on behalf of the Trump supporter playing along).

Note: It is again important to mention that Trump has not, to date, killed millions of people across several countries. However, it is important to note that his policies and path to power do follow suit with the much hated Dictator. Trump and Hitler are not the same person, nor is Trump some reincarnation of Hitler.

But, then again, even Hitler didn't start out a mass murderer guilty of numerous war crimes. He started out a vegetarian painter who rose to power and believed in relatively unproven ideas; like the invincibility power that came along with possessing the Spear of Destiny. Conversely, Trump was one of the loudest voices in the Birther movement; and he has called for some fairly disturbing tactics that would also break international law and be considered war crimes.

On to the game!

1. "Beauty and elegance, whether in a woman, a building, or a work of art, is not just superficial or something pretty to see."
2. "The world belongs to the man with guts!"
3. "Good people don't go into government."
4. "It is not the neutrals or the luke-warms who make history."
5. "In the end, you're not measured by how much you undertake, but by what you finally accomplish."
6. "Success is the sole earthly judge of right and wrong."
7. "The _____ has always been a people with definite racial characteristics..."
8. "My _____ has become so powerful that I can actually make my enemies tell the truth."
9. "The more economic difficulties increase, the more immigration will be seen as a burden."
10. Do not compare yourself to others. If you do so, you are insulting yourself."
11. "When women kill children-it's anything but murder: it is 'her right to choose.'"
12. "How fortunate for governments that the people...don't think."

Trump Game Answers

?	Answer
1	Trump
2	Hitler
3	Trump
4	Hitler
5	Trump
6	Hitler
7	Hitler
8	Trump
9	Hitler
10	Hitler
11	Hitler
12	Hitler

Final Thoughts

A phrase that is being used more and more frequently, as the Presidential Election moves from Primary season to General Election season, is that voters have a "choice between the lesser of two evils." It may come as no surprise that the writer of this book, along with Hyde Park Publishing, do not find Clinton to be an "evil." Trump is a proven liar, cheat, and misogynist who is hyper-sensitive to any criticism. Clinton is a dedicated public servant who has achieved a great deal of progress for women, children, the poor, and other underserved groups.

While Clinton may not be perfect, and her policies do evolve over time, that evolution is always in the direction of more inclusion. Clinton does not move against minorities, ethnic groups, world religions, and the most vulnerable. While Trump is proud of his ideals of disapproval, deriding, and derogation.

The slogan, "Make American Great Again" conjures a belief that America is no longer great. That at some time in the recent past, America has fallen from greatness and into failure. Trump has often said that America never wins anymore – at trade, negotiating, you name it. Trump's purported view is that America is a failure; and only by going back to when America "was great," can we move forward.

To any Trump supporters who may have read this far, take a moment to think through that concept.

Going back means slavery, suffrage, discrimination based on religion, race, creed, sexual orientation, gender, and a whole host more evils we have moved beyond as a society. It means the Great Depression and snake oil salesmen. Going back is the opposite of progress.

The straight, white man is a shrinking demographic in the overall makeup of the United States. The thoughts, prejudices, and values of the ruling class of most of the developed world is fading. While rich, straight, white men are still in a great many positions of power, that control topples a bit more each year. Resistance to Obama, and now Clinton, are public displays of the cultural revolution that has been happening for decades. And those who are the most adamantly against Obama, and now Clinton, rarely have substantive reasons (using facts) to oppose the progress. "He's a secret muslim" and "He's unqualified" partnered with "I don't know why but I just can't trust her" and "She shoulda done better with her husband's needs" are hallmark attacks.

Like any great empire, this demographic can either find a way to survive moving forward, or it can cling to power, lose everything, and become a self-harming sociopath longing for the days gone by.

And yes, sociopath is an apt term for what America is becoming under the tightening, but failing, grip of those like Trump.

SO·CI·O·PATH
noun
A person with a personality disorder manifesting itself in extreme
antisocial attitudes and behavior and a lack of conscience

www.ingramcontent.com/pod-product-compliance
Lightning Source LLC
Chambersburg PA
CBHW030534290526
45786CB00004B/1718